THE
ZODIAC
PROJECT

mdg-consultants.com

bluematrix.org

THE ZODIAC PROJECT

"We are all perfect, we are all masters"
— **Kenny Werner**, jazz pianist/jazz composer

Table of Contents

I. Introduction

Prologue

As you begin to read this book, I'd like you to keep an open mind, as this is not a traditional book. I'd like you to ask yourself to evaluate your life. More specifically, I'd like you to ask yourself if you are happy?

Of course, your definition of happiness will depend upon who you are — but do you have a sense of peace in your heart, a feeling of security about your future, and a feeling of anticipation when you wake up in the morning? If we can call this happiness, then would you say at this moment you are happy?

I think I can safely say that not that many people will be able to reply with a resounding yes. Most people are unable to say their life is everything they had hoped it would be. What is it that causes us so much unhappiness? What is it that is going on in the world that prevents so many people from simply being happy?

Well, it seems to me that we are living in an age of chaos. Chaos defined as a condition of confusion, indicative of unorganized matter (energy) that existed before the creation of the cosmos.

Simply by going about our lives, we find ourselves worn out and fatigued. Media, newspapers and television bombard us with information, and at work, we face problems and misunderstandings. The sources of our problems seem numerous and overwhelming.

This is likely to be the fact no matter where in the world we are likely to go. This tiny planet of ours is covered with economic conflict, domestic discord, religious wars, ethnic prejudice, environmental distress, and every other type of problem imaginable. And all the bad news about people suffering, people enjoying suffering, people getting richer, people getting poorer, the oppressed and the oppressors, reaches us in a matter of seconds from the opposite side of the globe.

Who? Might we ask, is responsible for all this suffering? The world is becoming an ever more divided, estranged, and complicated place to live. We are already up to our necks in chaos, but the world's troubles seem to be getting deeper and deeper.

One thing we all have in common is that we are all looking for a solution. Everyone is looking for an answer — and it is an answer that is so simple and effective that it has heretofore eluded us.

So what is the cause of all this chaos? What is the center of it all? Perhaps this is an inevitable phenomenon. Though we all belong to the same species, if we live in different places and in different cultures, the way we think is bound to be different.

And to make matters worse, most people have difficulty accepting things that are unlike the things around them. The result is a never-ending process of troubles and suffering. It would seem as long as people are people, any solution proposed is certain to come up short.

And so now we are back where we started. Can there ever be a single solution that can apply to all people on the globe, that everyone can be convinced of, and that is so simple that everyone can understand it?

An answer: "Energy"

In fact, I would like to propose an answer, and it is just this: We are nothing more than an assemblage of different types of energies, or molecules. We exist, from the moment we are conceived in our mothers' womb until we pass onto to another life, as energy.

From a physical perspective, humans are energy. When I first realized this I started to look at the world in a whole new way.

I realized that this connection to energy applies to all people, and, what I am about to propose in this book can be applied to everyone, all over the world. I believe it is also a way to start to see the way that people should live their lives.

So how can people live happy and healthy lives?

Energy that is moving is like water in a river, it remains pure because it is moving, when energy becomes trapped, like water, it ceases to flourish. Therefore, energy must be constantly moving. When this energy stops moving, the body starts to decay and if the energy stops in your brain, it can be life threatening.

But why does are energy become stagnant? We can think of it as a condition of stagnation of our emotions. Modern researchers have shown that the condition of the mind has a direct impact on the condition of the body. When you are living a full and enjoyable life, you feel better physically, and when your life is filled with struggles and sorrow, your body knows it — you can feel it.

Moving, changing, flowing —
this is what life is about — energy.

So what is this *"energy"*?

One answer might be that it is a life force, since it flows through our bodies and minds. In the same way water serves as the transporter of energy throughout our bodies (our bodies are 70% water). Energy circulates through our bodies and also circulates around the globe, flowing and moving at epic proportions. Hence, it explains the ocean tides, wind and weather, volcanoes, the gravitational pull of the planets, etc.

To understand energy is to understand ourselves, the cosmos, the marvels of nature, and life itself.

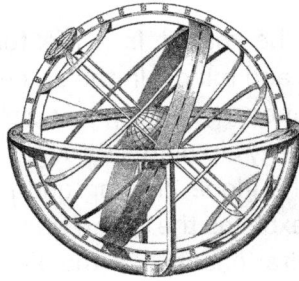

II. What is "The Zodiac Project"?

It occurred to me while living in Paris between the years 2004–2012, that an idea about this concept of "energy" could be intrinsically linked to the "Zodiac"; with all the interest worldwide in astrological signs and the phenomenon about "spiritual energy"; and might somehow have relevance in terms of my own personal, artistic, self discovery.

At the time, I was teaching architecture at well-known private university and attending two jazz music conservatories. I had gone to Paris to develop and explore some compositional and arranging ideas for an upcoming CD/DVD music project.

As I explored and conceptualized for this next project, one idea, centered around the word Zodiac, just wouldn't go away, the more I thought about it, researched it, and discussed it with my growing group of artists, creatives, astrologers, and continued to work on my music project (which, was at the time, now completely without focus... growing from just one CD project to five... standards, ballads, blues, latin, groove... ok, I thought... "I'll name it "Repertoire!"... I was just rationalizing with myself, the project was clearly without direction).

However, as each day passed... I kept coming back to a very simple concept theme that I believed had incredible artistic and potential... — "energy"... **The Zodiac.**

Finally, **"The Zodiac Project"** concept was conceived. (The moment it was conceived: i. e. the official moment... 12 midnight, on May 12, 2005, has been recorded in a short film — *"The Zodiac Project: One: Jazz — Parrallel Universe"*, which is described in one of following chapters in detail).

Zodiac, Greek origins?

I also discovered that that the word **Zodiac** means *"Cycle of Life"*, from the Greek word: **"ZOE"**; which means *"life"*, and the word: **"DIAC"**, which means *"cycle"*, and coincidentally (I wasn't quite ready to think it was spiritual connection that made this possible...) it soon became very apparent to me that everything in my own life was somehow symbolically, mystically and explainable relative to the number "12".

All of life's energy can be understood in terms of "12"?

Twelve signs, twelve musical notes (which, I had already been struggling to integrate into my soul for about 15 years of playing professional jazz), twelve colours (these are also related to the signs and musical notes), etc.

And coincidentally enough, I was also born on the 12th of May (which makes me a Taurus, and what was that all about?) More about that later.

Now, I was really curious if there was strange "energy" connection to explain all of this and my life... (perhaps, it was destiny?)

I'll let the record of my life (so far) speak for itself...

For some reason, all of sudden, after 51 years (now 58) of really not understanding who I was and, what my life all about... I happened (by accident?) to stumble upon an approach to seriously focus my own energy via various, but related, artistic mediums — which are detailed in the pages that follow.

I suppose I have somewhat of a talent for each of these mediums — because they come rather easily (albeit, I have to do all the work) and as such, I was able to put them together into this book.

The Zodiac Framework: "Energy Map"

As a direct result of thinking about my own life in these terms, I have developed what I have termed: **"The Zodiac Framework"**, or, what I have also termed an: **"ENERGY MAP"**.

And during it's development, I became aware this framework, or "Energy Map", had tremendous applications for an even more "holistic" approach. or, as shall I call it: *wayfinding*, whereby, other people just as I did, might find their own "way" (i. e. their own "cycle of life" or, purpose, or understanding of who they are) and perhaps, gain understanding into their own life's journey.

Potential

I then started to imagine the possibilities, (of not only the first musical part) if this project was executed professionally and connected with like-minded individuals, coming from all walks of life, creative, business, social, scientific, adminstratiive, patrons, etc. who could support the concept and believe in it's merit. Enough so, that they are willing to participate on many different levels to see this concept is successful and mindful of their unique contributions.

Subsequently this book was developed.

Still with me?

I know it gets abstract, but in truth, that is part of the beauty of this book.

The abstraction, actually makes it even more attractive. I prefer not to use the word abstract, but "mystical". — It was here all along... for all of us to discover, understand and believe in.

Why have so many millions placed their faith in religion? A belief? I would propose The Zodiac Concept, which is based on some rather fundelmental principles from the scientific and psychological disciplines... is far easier to comprehend and believe in than even the teachings of religion.

Two ideas to consider

The French newspaper *"Figaro"* printed an article (April 25th, 2005) commenting on the possible linkages in astrology. The article highlighted the connections between the psychological and scientific worlds. The *Figaro* is known worldwide a very conservative, right wing newspaper. Publishing such an article illustrates the growing public interest and debate that exists about this topic.

Second, hardly a day goes by where you don't personally hear someone ask: "What's your sign?" or, "Did you read your horoscope today?" or, in a quiet moment, do you see people stare into space and wondering about their life, their meaning... Am I wrong? Don't you do this?

The main point here is that, it is already a topical issue, with an extremely large population of people who are already interested a various levels of involvement.

But it's more than that...

Remember this phrase:
"We are all masters and we are all perfect"
(note: this phrase will be repeated often in throughout this book)

We are already "perfect", we are already "masters"... we need only explore our energy and the universes' energy to truly understand how this life force is at the very core of our search for happiness.

As for me, I know my contribution

I am an artist who has choosen to explore this concept for my own lifes' work, and I sincerely think there are (countless) others who will feel equally motivated to support the effort, and find applications to their own life questions and self-discovery.

All good news, but one step at a time...

The Zodiac Project: A Unique Concept

There is currently no similar book completed that is based on the same fundamental principles. The Zodiac Projects' 12-part, artistic wayfinding platform, that not only provides a vehicle for development of one's own inner energy, but helps transform your life journey and understand significant decision milestones... and why?

How this concept is presented?

The entire book is presented with each part of the 12 parts written to involve notable and world famous artists, collaborators and creatives in each of the respective art fields.

All of the preceeding are fundelmental keys to the success of the Zodiac Project.

Current Snapshot

As I mentioned, the concept for the Zodiac Project originated in February 2005, in Paris, France, and, the fundamental concept model remains, but most assuredly will undergo enhancements and revisions over time.

After extensive research, I have modeled and developed an overall framework, or, "Energy Map" for self-discovery by analyzing my own "cycle of life", i. e.: spiritual energy and artistic journey, and have developed this framework for others. Other similar projects aligned with this concept of the energy map might be: "The Artists Way" or, "What Color is my Parachute".

Examples of my life parts are included and developed for each of the 12 parts.

III. Zodiac Elements and Principles

The Zodiac Project has been uniquely developed to explore the essence of the twelve Zodiac Signs, with the four energy elements: air, water, earth and fire, as well as the principle relationships aligned with the seasons: winter, spring, summer and fall. These have been researched and developed from both Western and Chinese astrological perspectives.

The essence of Chinese Astrology has been incorporated in The Zodiac Project to reinforce the principles and inter-relationships of the theories and premises presented in the underlying philosophical framework ("wayfinding") for the twelve signs and twelve project parts.

As we learn more about our own life by thinking of it in these terms, the end result is an "Energy Map", which is described and outlined in the 12 Parts of The Zodiac Project. (Note: Illustrated in this book is mine, to demonstrate the application of the theory and premises behind these principles and relationships).

But first...

What is the zodiac?
And why does it have a relationship to "Energy"?

Briefly, the astrological zodiac is divided into 12 signs, each 30 degrees long. The cycle of zodiac signs starts with Aries, which begins at the spot on the ecliptic where the Sun is on the first day of spring. These 30-degree sections of the sky are actually blocks of space, not time.

Zodiac signs are often confused in the popular mind with "sun signs". When a person says, "I'm an Aries!" what they're really saying is they were born at a time of the year when the Sun is in the zodiac sign of Aries. Because our calendar is designed to mimic the motions of the Sun around the zodiac, the Sun is in Aries at nearly the same time period each year (roughly March 20th or 21st to April 19th or 20th). Hence the 12 sun signs are like months of a calendar based on the zodiac. They represent time, not space.

The motions of the other planets through the zodiac signs can be quite irregular, compared to the Sun's motion. On average, they range from the fast moving Moon (which spends about 2–1/2 days in each sign) to the slow poke Pluto (roughly 12 to 24 years in each sign).

Planetary Rulers of the Signs

Each sign is associated with a planet that is called the "ruler" of that sign. Usually, there is some similarity in meaning or energy between the sign and its ruler. A planet is supposed to express its energy in the most natural, straightforward fashion through the sign it rules.

Some signs (Scorpio, Aquarius, and Pisces) have two rulers, an old, traditional ruler and a modern one. Since the discovery of Uranus, Neptune, and Pluto the last few centuries, these planets have replaced the traditional rulers. And with the introduction of Chiron and the major asteroids into astrology, yet another round of arguments about rulers is breaking out. Perhaps the entire notion of "rulership" should be taken with a grain of salt.

Sub-Cycle Symbolism

Although a certain amount of mythology is associated with the meanings of each sign, most of these meanings are actually derived by looking at the zodiac as a collection of overlapping cycles within cycles.

For instance, the cycle of the 4 elements (fire, earth, air, and water) describes 4 different personality types. This cycle is repeated 3 times around the zodiac.

The 3 modalities (cardinal, fixed, mutable) establish 3 distinct styles of expressing energy; this cycle is repeated 4 times. Very similar to the way that there are 4 seasons: Winter, Spring, Summer and Fall.

Each sign has a polarity (positive/negative, or in the older texts, masculine/feminine) that alternates with each sign.

Further, the zodiac is divided into thirds (primordial, individual, and universal) and halves (subjective, objective), which suggests a life cycle of growing emotional and social maturation.

The interweaving of all these sub-cycles then creates the overall profile of the zodiac sign.

There are interpretations of the Zodiac Signs in terms of both Western and Chinese Astrology. Colors, symbols and musical note are somewhat different for each astrology approach, but not surprisingly, both have direct application to the development of The Zodiac Project.

What is interesting is that there are 3 "givens" for the "core" concept of the "Energy Map": (1) sign, (2) color and (3) musical note and then there are 9 "unknowns" to discover (i. e. how? what? when? where? why? etc) just as there are 9 planets to discover their affect on your energy path. I call it the framework for the "wayfinding" principle.

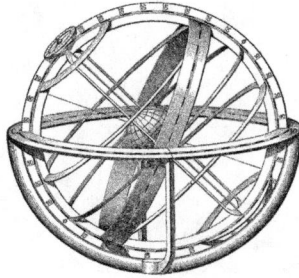

IV. Twelve Zodiac Signs

ARIES

Ruler	Mars
Element	Fire
Mode	Cardinal
Pole	Positive
Third	Primordial
Half	Subjective
Color	Red-Orange
Musical Note	C

Unbridled expression of your inner nature; activity that is self-motivated, unaffected by others; new beginnings, "the start of new cycles", birth; enthusiasm and vitality.

Aggressive, willful, powerful, assertive; enthusiastic about whatever interests you at the moment, focused in short bursts, unlikely to sustain interest in the long term; ego expression; adventurous, pioneering; Warrior-type energy; impatient with having to cooperate with others, works best alone or in leadership role; unconcerned with approval or acceptance; lacks persistence and stamina; honest and forthright, "what you see is what you get", not given to airs or pretenses; the first expression (or incarnation) of spirit within a new cycle on the physical plane.

Aries traditionally begins the astrological year, i. e.: on March 21st, there are equal parts of night and day. When you do an "Energy Map" for your specific life journey, you reset the 0 degree plane to your sign for that same day, (i. e. "first breathe" of your own energy cycle (since that specific day (when you are borne into this world) has equal parts night and day — more about that later).

Every 3 days there are spectrum variations in the color for each sign, a total of 10 spectral color energies per zodiac sign. i. e. Aires begin with a pure "hue" of red with small amounts of "chromatic" characteristics of orange, gradually as the degrees pass (days), the hue of red is more saturated with orange chroma.

TAURUS

Ruler	Venus
Element	Earth
Mode	Fixed
Pole	Negative
Third	Primordial
Half	Subjective
Color	Green-Gold
Musical Note	F

Grounding, bringing down to earth; constancy, steadiness, fixedness; spirit becoming embodied, entering matter, taking on a form; a vessel or container for spiritual forces.

Earthy, grounded, in touch with the body; sensual, pleasure seeking; stubborn, fixed, stands their ground; focuses and concentrates energy, gives it concrete expression, practical, provides stamina and persistence; slow, steady, methodical; fertile, productive; unreflective, content to simply be; spirit becoming involved with the material world.

Clearly, from this artist's standpoint the key sign in the cycle of life (Zodiac) is Taurus, (as well as the Taurean inter-relationships within The Zodiac Project) in as much it is this artist's sign, not surprisingly the beginning of my journey, (from a spiritual sense), began on the Twelfth of May.

This entire project and the framework that has been developed for the Framework Energy Map for others is also based on this fundamental structure: 12.

GEMINI

Ruler	Mercury
Element	Air
Mode	Mutable
Pole	Positive
Third	Primordial
Half	Subjective
Color	Blue-Yellow
Musical Note	Bb

Curiosity, cleverness, skill, communication; making connections with surroundings, trying to "figure things out"; the first display of intelligence by embodied spirit.

Talkative ("a Gemini is born with a telephone in each hand!"), communicative, sociable; loves to interact with others (at least on a superficial level); unemotional, impersonal, ruled by "rationality"; requires great mental and sometimes physical stimulation, curious to a fault; playful, "the Trickster", the Devil's Advocate; changeable, inconstant, attention easily drifts to something new, seeks novelty.

CANCER

Ruler	Moon
Element	Water
Mode	Cardinal
Pole	Negative
Third	Primordial
Half	Subjective
Color	Blue-Pink
Musical Note	Eb

Nurturing, support, belonging, emotional bonds; your roots, source, ground of your being; the unconscious, feelings, emotion; "the Great Mother", Universal Womb; spirit's first emotional attachments to the world.

Mothering, emotional and physical nurturance; experiences and imprinting during infancy and childhood; family, ancestors, heritage, relationships to the past; belonging, feeling "at home"; maternal love, caring; feeling supported by the world, that your needs are provided for; insecurities and fears if your needs haven't been fulfilled; possessiveness, "twisted love", inability to nurture others are negative expressions.

LEO

Ruler	Sun
Element	Fire
Mode	Fixed
Pole	Positive
Third	Individual
Half	Subjective
Color	Yellow
Musical Note	Ab

Spirit entering the realm of the individual person; ego development, setting yourself apart from the rest of the world, becoming your own person; self-expression, being true to your inner nature, acting from the heart; dawning awareness of self in relation to others.

Ego, self-centered, arrogant; fixed, stubborn, persistent; artistic or creative expression as a vehicle for revealing "who I am"; needs to be a center of attention, requires acknowledgment and approval, likes to be noticed and appreciated ("ego-strokes"); personal integrity, true to self, honorable, trustworthy; kingly, self-assured, confident.

VIRGO

Ruler	Mercury
Element	Earth
Mode	Mutable
Pole	Negative
Third	Individual
Half	Subjective
Color	Yellow-Brown
Musical Note	Db

Embodiment of the individual in the world; problems of adjustment dealing with the world and others; perfection of your approach to life, development of mundane skills; ability to change to adapt to life better.

Service, helping, self-effacing; perfectionist, always seeking to improve, efficiency; practical, functional, interested in crafts and projects; true to self in a simple, unassuming manner; reacts to defeats and setbacks by pulling back and altering approach, lacks confidence in the face of opposition; lives up to duties and responsibilities; interested in maintaining the body as a fit vehicle; diet, exercise, herbs, etc.; aware of conflicts with others, of the give and take required by life.

LIBRA

Ruler	Venus
Element	Air
Mode	Cardinal
Pole	Positive
Third	Individual
Half	Objective
Color	Blue
Musical Note	Gb

Spirit as individual entering into relationship with others; partnership, one-to-one relationships, meeting others as an equal, interdependency; encountering repressed parts of yourself through others (via projection); going beyond ego boundaries; peace, harmony, balance; social awareness.

Partners, marriage; learning how to get along peaceably with others, treating others as equals; "I vs. You", conflict, enemies; art, beauty, harmonious surroundings; distressed by stressful, inharmonious interactions; intimacy; people in counseling professions.

SCORPIO

Ruler	Pluto
Element	Water
Mode	Fixed
Pole	Negative
Third	Individual
Half	Objective
Color	Light Blue
Musical Note	B

Transformation, change, ego-death, rebirth, transcendence; intense emotional involvement with the process of personal growth; movement from individual certainties to the "mysteries of life"; spirit breaking through the limitations of individual ego.

Intense, passionate, brooding, magnetic; stubborn, unyielding, driven by emotions; stands up for self, usually covertly, manipulates power; understands deeper layers of the psyche beyond the ego, unable to communicate this well leading to misunderstandings; intrigued by the "dark side" of life; the underground, people whose job involves going beneath surface appearances; sexuality, especially the transformative power of the orgasm; self-mastery, breaking free of illusory limitations, the Hero.

SAGITTARIUS

Ruler	Jupiter
Element	Fire
Mode	Mutable
Pole	Positive
Third	Universal
Half	Objective
Color	Yellow-Red
Musical Note	E

Spirit moving beyond the realm of the individual into the world at large; becoming a member of a wider society; experiences that lead to consciousness expansion, being receptive to new points of view, wisdom, enlightenment; using your talents for the benefit of the greater whole.

Freedom loving, idealist, unfettered by "small thinking"; inspiration; religion, philosophy, the law; awareness of your connections to the rest of the world; can be distant from others, afraid to give up freedom, reluctant to be tied down; on the other hand, aware of the value of the social contract; enthusiastic, gregarious, generous; loves abstract, theoretical ideas, sees the big picture, ignores the details; in love with an ideal; foreign travel, liberating experiences.

CAPRICORN

Ruler	Saturn
Element	Earth
Mode	Cardinal
Pole	Negative
Third	Universal
Half	Objective
Color	Brown
Musical Note	A

Spirit's attempt to bring about the perfect society, to create heaven on earth; making practical, efficient connections with others on the physical plane; ambitious, feels pride in accomplishments; concern with truth, reality, "hard facts"; relationship to authority.

Serious, determined, disciplined, focused; needs to play more; fathering, disciplining love; authority figures; seeks certainties in life, wants things "cast in concrete"; the Businessman, concerned with the practical relationships to support yourself within society; not interested in "blue sky" ideas, needs to bring theory into concrete reality; "knowing the rules and playing the game"; making a niche in the world.

AQUARIUS

Ruler	Uranus
Element	Air
Mode	Fixed
Pole	Positive
Third	Universal
Half	Objective
Color	Medium Blue
Musical Note	D

Spirit's attempt to create ideal relationships and organizations, based on freedom and cooperation between individuals; freethinking, unorthodox, not shackled by outdated ideology; the perfection of society.

Even though ideas are often far-sighted, they can be held and expressed in rigid, dogmatic fashion (this is a fixed sign, afterall!); "everyone should be free to be just like me!"; idealistic, utopian; derives sense of identity from groups and their goals, tends to dominate them; impersonal thinking, detached from emotional considerations; produces "humanitarian without compassion"; friendships based on common goal.

PISCES

Ruler	Neptune
Element	Water
Mode	Mutable
Pole	Negative
Third	Universal
Half	Objective
Color	Dark Blue
Musical Note	G

Surrender to the universe, to higher goals; ego sacrifice; compassion and empathy, selfless work; seeing the unity of all things; the ends of cycles, forming "seeds" for the next cycle of growth; spirit as individual dissolving back into pure spirit.

Mysticism, escape into the One; sees the unity, fails to make "normal" distinctions, often weak ego; victim, martyr, servant; tends to escapism, fantasy, drugs (especially alcohol), religion; very receptive, sensitive, even psychic; co-dependency, care-taking; withdrawn from the world; release from the world. The last sign in the Zodiac cycle, the end of the Zodiac year. And also a "mix" of all the previous 11 energies. Think about a Pisces person you know... true?

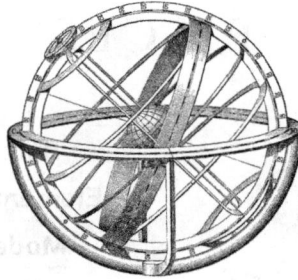

V. The Parallel Universe —
The "Conscious vs Subconscious"

What is our purpose?
The meaning for our life journey?

Remember: *"we are all perfect... we are all masters"*
— **Kenny Werner**, jazz pianist/jazz composer

I would like to propose as one of the basic premises for The
Zodiac Project, that there is another energy, or, "Universe"
(one that exists on a parallel plane) co-existing with the one we
live in day-to-day, this psychological "space", where everyone
is subconsciously searching for meaning of their life, journey
and purpose. My contention is that this subconscious plane,the
one that is "influenced" by the various energies around us, i.
e. the energy of our planet, the energy related to the day we
started our journey (birthdate), the movement of the planets
and the energy of those around us. It's the plane that main-
tains our resolve, where we find inspiration, the place we go

when we search inside, where we feel, where we try to connect, where lives change, where decisions and ideas are made and formulated, where we begin our thoughts that later turn to actions, where we cherish our experiences, hopes and dreams... This subconscious plane can better understood and explored by thinking about it as "energy", and discovering and using tools associated with some fundamental concepts related to astrology and spirituality-both scientific and psychological.

How the "cycle of life" begins

Let's face it, we begin with just one breathe and when the time comes, we end with just one breathe... so isn't it our responsibility at some level to connect our conscious actions and (perhaps decisions) with our subconscious needs and desires?

Psychologists have studied this "sense of actualization" for many reasons, i. e.: to understand our hierarchies of needs, and why people search for and seek "Inner Peace"? (you know... those moments of anxiety, the restlessness... "what am I doing?")

The Zodiac Project presents an alternative approach to understanding life's meaning.

For each of us, the pursuit will be different...

For me, it was to "find" myself as an artist. For each of us it's different. It's a process to connect the subconscious with the conscious. The "wayfinding energy map" shows you how to look at your life in these terms.

I hope you will enjoy your journey of discovery as much as I have enjoyed mine.

What is the Zodiac Philosophy?

Question: What have we become?

Answer: "Business-oriented, materialistic, chaos, robots, unthinking, catatonic world, lack of humanity, sincerity, sensibility..."

People are always thinking, evaluating, and analyzing their own past, present and future, and I contend are always looking at their own cycle of life, either subconsciously or consciously, perhaps to find their own purpose, to understand better their lives and those around them... their actions, their beliefs.

The Zodiac Project philosophy explores the spiritual, symbolic, mystical, and artistic journey for the "meaning of life", and strives to provide a framework to facilitate people to (re) build their lives by connecting to a "Parallel Universe" (a spiritual world), with fundelmental values connected to culture, harmony, art, history, religious, psychological and emotional needs, emphasizing sensitivity and creativity.

Another question: At the present time: What are our life values?

Answer: "Me, myself and I".
And finally, what do I mean by "Parallel Universe"?

I would define it as traveling inside oneself to (re)discover our own true values first, and then (re)visiting the essence of our lives and purpose. Once we have done that, we open up to the possibility of our spirituality and our energy.

Let me try to explain it another way:

Metaphorically (linked to astrology)... think of it as the "known" — conscious reality, i. e. the existing 9 planets in the solar system, and the "unknown", or "subconscious" plane, or, perhaps the 3 yet undiscovered planets (or in this context: the "me, myself and I") and so, as illustrated in the "wayfinding" framework, these are the "given" parts for each person, i. e. (1) your sign, and (2) the corresponding color and (3) musical note. As we explore our life energy through the Zodiac Process ("Energy Map"), we discover our real selves, in this ways our other 9 parts. All of which equals 12. Because we are discovering ourselves in this "parrallel plane" the relationships are opposite. (Because the parrellel universe exists like a mirror, reflecting all relationships relative to energy with their corresponding polar opposite)

Understanding this principal is critical to understanding the application of the Zodiac Project framework.

This is summarized as:
Conscious Plane: (reality)
9 knowns
3 unknowns

Sub-Conscious Plane: ("Energy Map")
3 knowns
9 unknowns

But how do we explore this energy?
Here's how I explored my energy...

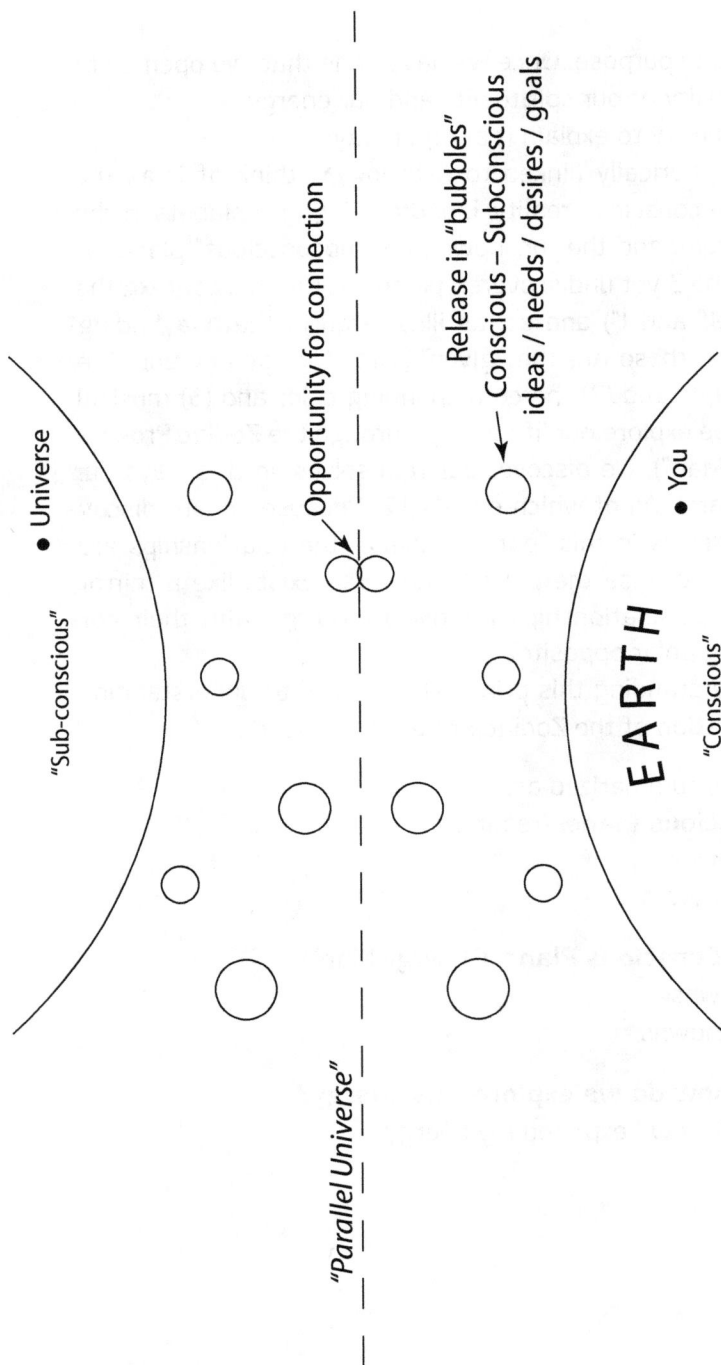

"Sub-conscious"

● Universe

Opportunity for connection

Release in "bubbles"
Conscious – Subconscious
ideas / needs / desires / goals

"Parallel Universe"

EARTH

"Conscious"

● You

Parallel Universe "The Conscious vs Subconcsious"
The Zodiac Project

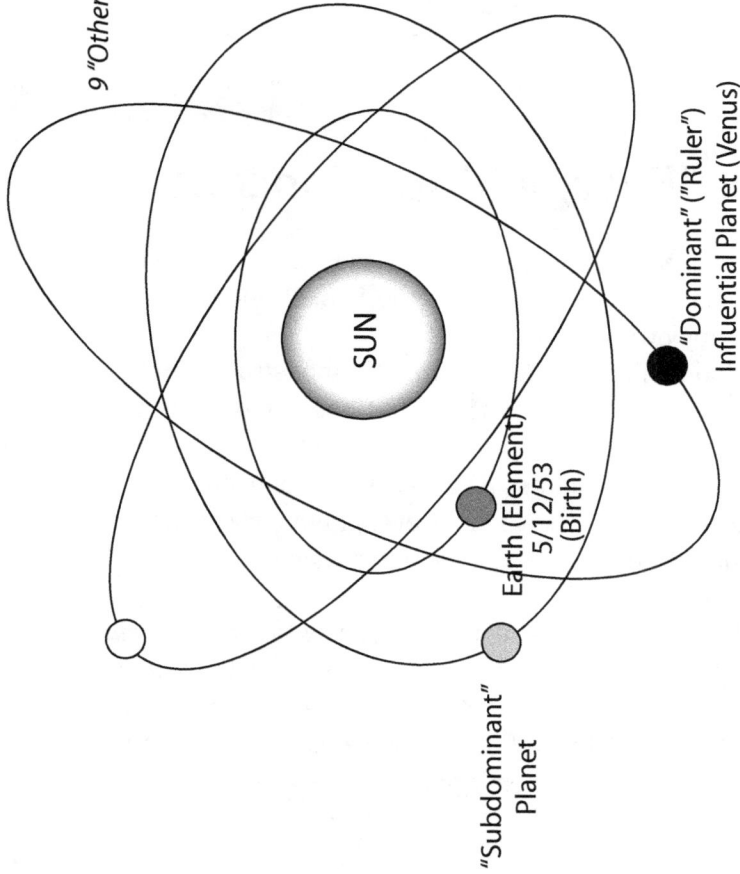

9 "Other" Planet Orbits

Planets revolving around the sun like an energy molecule

SUN

Earth (Element)
5/12/53
(Birth)

"Dominant" ("Ruler")
Influential Planet (Venus)

"Subdominant" Planet

Ruler : Venus
Element: Earth
Mode: Fixed
Pole: Negative
Third: Primordial
Half: Subjective
Color: Green-Cold
Musical Note : F

My Zodiac Sign: "Energy Map"
The Zodiac Project

VI. "Energy Map" Concept

My own energy cycle began on the 12th of May, 1953 (Chinese Astrology: year of the Snake) and so, the beginning of my own life journey...

The Zodiac Project includes this "Demonstration Project" (as I like to term it) which is modeled on one persons' life experience, awareness and exploration-mine. I will outline and present in twelve art mediums, my own keys to connecting to this "Parallel Universe". The universe of every humans' essence-our energy, our spirituality. The connection between subconscious and conscious.

The basic premise is that "everyone" is already a *"master"* and *"perfect"*... and merely has to connect with their own "Parallel Universe" and potential. And the way we do this is by exploring the scientific and psychological connections of this spiritual and astrological "energy".

12 Parts of "The Zodiac Project"

The Energy Map illustrates how different energies, signs, colours, etc. are analyzed and identified to define/illustrate a life journey.

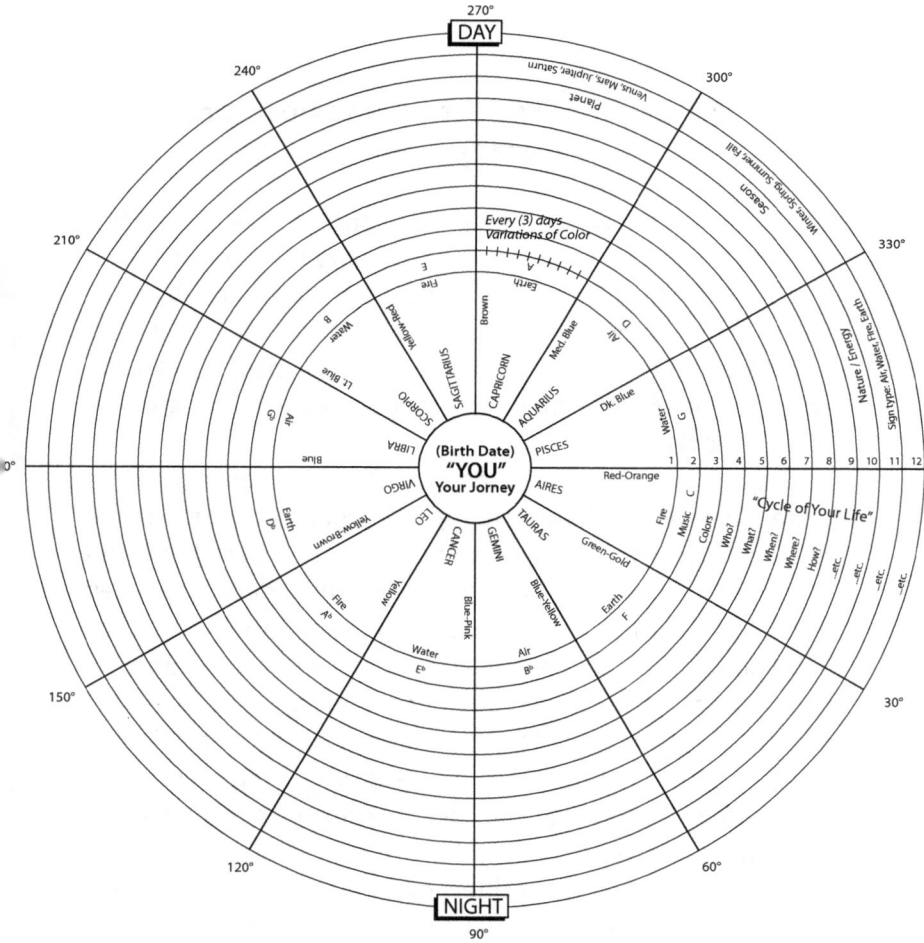

You and me... it's all about energy!

I have spent 50 years wondering about the "WHY?" of my life.. "what was my purpose? "Why did my journey include music, architecture, painting, writings, poetry, traveling, color, (and seemingly) many different (albeit artistic) directions...

The Zodiac Project Framework or, "Energy Map"

As a result of these questions and considerable research, I was able to develop an kind of evolutionary life framework, or, an **"ENERGY MAP"** i. e., a process/framework for discovering my own purpose and life journey. This study resulted in an "methodology" that could be utilized by all people, all signs, regardless of whether they were men or women, young or old, etc. all over the world.

This "Energy Map" became a approach to develop a step-by-step method, or, **"Wayfinding"** for everyone to understand their own lives, build an awareness of their own **"Parallel Universe"** (a universe that influences their decisions, their interactions with people, and quite possibly their reactions to particular events) and, may even result in fundamental life changes. (For example: this became part of my own way-finding and resulted in the music composition, titled: "Course Change"). The objective akin to the psychological heirarchy of becoming self-actualized, and therefore, to link the sub-conscious and conscious lives for eternity. (Note: psychology theory suggests that this achievement produces an incredible feelings of deep life fullfillment or, happiness once you feel this way about your life... Remember: "we are already masters, we are already perfect").

So let's begin to really focus on the meaning of this project...

- What is the "Cycle of Life?"
- What is all this talk about "Energy"?
- How many times do you hear: "What's your sign?"

Let's take a small journey, imagine for a moment...

You are standing up in front of an audience of 4,500 people and your mouth is around a strange tube of metal with holes in it, and then imagine, there are four other people (musicians) interacting with similar strange, sound-emitting devices.

How is music created in that moment? Technology? Luck? Education? Experience? Or a combination of all these, or, something else?

Is it a connection, or another language? Why is art art? Why does it makes us feel and react a certain way? What do our life experiences, chronological age, mood and psychological space have to do with it? Haven't we all thought or imagined some other world, the world beyond here and now at some point in our lives? Why do we even care about our energy, our sign, our birthdate?

I think it's because we all have the same underlying questions and thoughts about life. And generally, don't these feelings arise when we listen to music?

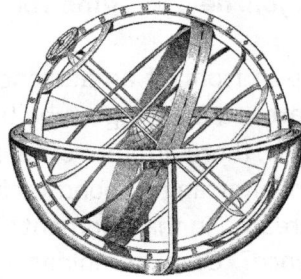

VII. My "Energy Map"

Part One — Jazz: "Parallel Universe"

Part Two — "Les Peintures"

Part Three — "Analogies in Architecture"

Part Four — "Reflections": Poems for Zodiac

Part Five — "Zodioconstructivisim": Sculpture

Part Six — "The Language": Writings

Part Seven — Cities: "The Earth Explored"

Part Eight — Photographs: "A Visual Essay"

Part Nine — Teachings and People

Part Ten — "Les Colours"

Part Eleven — "Les Femmes"

Part Twelve — The Zodiac Project Foundation

Here are "my" (12) Twelve "Energy Map" Parts: 3 which are given for each person: sign, color, musical note, and 9, which I "discovered" through this "wayfinding" process.

My "Energy Map" (under construction)

This section of the Book continues to be added to and re-vised as it will include the history of my musical journey (CDs, DVDs, Concerts, etc.) architecture, career, educational journey and development, etc... and how and why the zodiac project idea came about.

I grew up in New Jersey (lived there for 17 years), moved to California in 1984, then moved to Paris in 2004, then went to Johns Hopkins University on a full fellowship, was married 11 years and now have a beautiful son, multi-faceted interna-tional artistic career (architecture, music, teaching, perform-ing, writing, modeling, etc.), conceived and managed internet businesses, competed in world championship athletics all over the world, and studied and lived in a variety of places and cul-tures, etc. Quite a journey so far...

Part One
Jazz: "Parallel Universe"

Subconscious Concept: Part One of my Zodiac Project consists of a contemporary jazz (instrumental and vocal) music CD and DVD. Each of the 12 jazz compositions musically interprets the energy of the zodiac signs, presenting a spiritual and musical life journey. Arrangements are presented in a mystical, symbolic "cycle of life" context, within the jazz music idiom.

Concious Reality: CD/DVD w/ 12 cover art paintings. (Note: similar examples of this music project concept would be *Norah Jones'* first album, or, how *SADE* has done any of her projects). Based on the approach that the individual compositions (12) and the entire CD take the listener to a place, or on a musical, spiritual journey as it relates to the cycle of life energy. i. e. from the beginning of life, when you take your first "Breathe" — Track One... until your spirit moves on and into the universe: "Eternity" — Track Twelve.

Compositions

Intro: *"Buzz"*
Concept: energy transfer decompression composition piece to transfer the listener's state of mind from the conscious to subconscious planes, i. e. think: prologue, introduction.

Trk 1. "Breathe"
Concept: heartbeat, birth, first relationship to our spiritual energy in our life.

Trk 2. "First Steps"
Concept: slow bluesy ballad, awakening.

Trk 3. "Nomad"
Concept: searching the physical world.

Trk 4. "Les Femmes Neurotique" or "Dreamgirl"
(*Les Hommes Neurotique* — for women)
Concept: attachments, adolescent love, first experiences.

Trk 5. "Discovery" (me, myself and I)
Concept: foundations of "Self".

Trk 6. "Evolution"
Concept: begin development of who we "are", our place in society.

Trk 7. "Time and Space"
Concept: awareness of world we live in, culture, relationship to other societies.

Trk 8. "Bubble Theory" (Blues)
Concept: hard driving, you have to first put the bubbles out if you truly want to connect.

Trk 9. "Solar Voyage"
Concept: your life goals, objectives, ideas, disembracement/ arrival

Trk 10. "Course Change"
Concept: personal realization, reconstruction, mid-life crisis? Life altering Event? Accident?

Trk 11. "Lost in Translation": Galaxy

Concept: transition phase: before we arrive at our self-actualization phase.

Trk 12 "Parallel Universe": "Eternity"

Concept: resolution, life 's mystery finds spiritual light.

"After Buzz"

Concept: energy transfer that returns the listener to conscious world.

Sampling of Music projects: (partial list)

Who Can I Turn To? 1998, (Blue Matrix Records) Jazz CD — standards inspired by loss of family member, friend, established "self" as only true identity.

Stolen Moments, 2000, (Blue Matrix Records) Jazz CD — standards inspired by spiritual journey of composer Oliver Nelson. (who wrote title track).

Out of Nowhere Band: Live In Concert, 2003, (Blue Matrix Records) DVD.

www.bluematrix.org

~

www.amazon.com/Philip-Gordon/e/B000APN8B8/

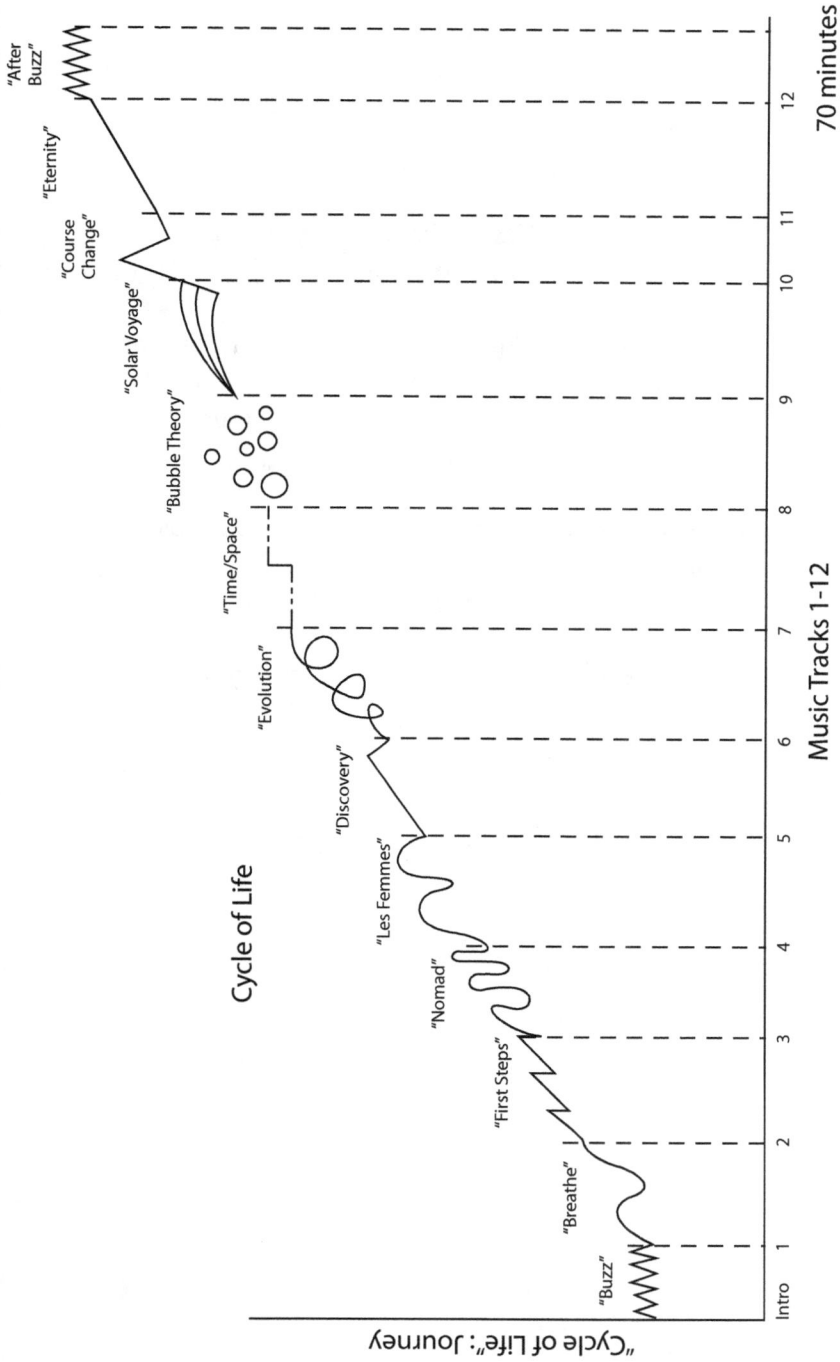

Concept: The Zodiac Project
Part One: Jazz "Parallel Universe"

Music Tracks 1-12

70 minutes

Cycle of Life

"Cycle of Life": Journey

"Buzz"
"Breathe"
"First Steps"
"Nomad"
"Les Femmes"
"Discovery"
"Evolution"
"Time/Space"
"Bubble Theory"
"Solar Voyage"
"Course Change"
"Eternity"
"After Buzz"

Intro 1 2 3 4 5 6 7 8 9 10 11 12

Part Two
"Les Peintures"

Subconscious Concept: Interpretation of the 12 Parts of the "Zodiac cycle of life" with a 12 canvas, acrylic painting format, with juxtapositions of music rhythms, colors, musical notes, signs, women, architecture, cities, etc...

Concious Reality: Paintings, Exhibitions, reproducibles, brochures, books, etc.

Actual Paintings: (12), size: 5'0" by 7'0", stretched canvas, with frames, color, acrylic.

See website: http://www.mdg-consultants.com

Part Three
"Analogies in Architecture"

Subconscious Concept: Over the period of approximately 30 years, I have worked internationally and professionally as an architect, interior designer, planner, lighting designer, instructor, writer and professor of Architecture. Completely significant, multi-disciplinary, multi-phase projects, ranging in size from $500,000 to $1.5 billion in construction value. I have designed and executed governmental, commercial, residential, corporate, retail projects worldwide. I was recognized by the San Francisco Archdiocese as the "Private Citizen Person Who Contributed the Most" in the year 2002 to the Catholic Church in SF.

Concious Reality: Video Essay of projects: DVD format and coffee table book with illustrations and text.

Detail: Each of the 12 projects chosen have a spiritual relationship to the 12 Zodiac signs, i. e.:

Sampling of Projects:

1. Hotels/Casinos: Las Vegas-Harrah's/MGM/The Reserve/ Lucky chances': Las Vegas, Nevada

2. Catholic Cathedral: Saint Patrick's: Menlo Park, California

3. Zen Centre: Paris, France

4. Airports: San Francisco International/BWI

5. Retail/Commercial: Prototypes

6. Large Scale Corporate Master Plan: Lockheed and IBM, San Jose, California

7. Custom Residences: Woodside and Palo Alto, California

8. Corporate Headquarters: Symantec, Cupertino, California

9. Corporate Interiors: Levi's European Headquarters, Paris, France

10. Exteriors: Falla Project: Palo Alto, California

11. Fantasy Architecture: Nautilus Islands, Sausilito, California

12. Research/Technology: Xerox Corporation (PARC) and Sun Microsystems, Palo Alto, California

Status: Twelve projects completed and selected, archiving in process.

See website http://www.mdg-consultants.com for additional project information and photo gallery and listings.

Part Four
"Reflections": Poems for the Zodiac

Subconscious Concept: Book of poetry with illustrations.

Concious Reality: A poetry book and on-line sketch illustrations, working titles follow the "cycle of life: i. e.

1. I'm a Man
2. Innocence
3. New Day
4. Alone Again
5. Individuals
6. Maybe
7. Our Energy, Our Love
8. If you were me
9. Run Love
10. One day
11. I
12. I am

Published 2011 Blue Matrix Productions.

www.bluematrix.org

~

www.amazon.com/Philip-Gordon-Reflections-
Selected-Poems/dp/0984763813

Part Five
"Zodiaconstructivisim": Sculpture

Subconscious Concept: Sculptures that interpret the "cycle of life" concept.

Concious Reality: Series of (12) sculptures, fabricated of marble, steel, glass, cast plaster, acrylic and machinery parts (6' 0" tall).

Sculptures:

1. *"Invitation"*: Located in Xerox (PARC) Lobby: Palo Alto, California (completed: 2001)

2. *"Inspiration"*: Located in Sun Microsystems Lobby, Palo Alto, California (completed: 2002)

3. *"Series I"*: Private Residence: Woodside, California (completed in 2002)

4. Sculptures 4-12. TBD (sketches in development)

3 sculptures finished, 5 maquettes prepared, design studies in process.

See website http://www.mdg-consultants.com for photographs of finished sculptures/related work.

Part Six
"The Language": Writings

Subconscious Concept: Collection of 12 significant writings completed by PG, dealing with topics of energy, life journey, life forces and cycle of life concepts.

Concious Reality: Books, publications, screenplay-movie, articles, poetry, letters, etc.

The Writings:

1. Screenplay: The Zodiac Project: *"Pendulum"* (Completed: 1990, synopsis — see appendix)

2. Magazine Article Front Cover Interview: *"Wayne Shorter: The Man and The Legacy"* (4 Grammies/jazz musician of the year). *Jazztimes* (Published 2003)

3. Book: *"Principles and Practices of Lighting Design: Art of Lighting Composition"*, Blue Matrix Productions (Published 2011)

4. Question and Answer column, *Real Estate Journal* "Inside Design and Development" (Monthly, 1996–2000)

5. Contributing Jazz Writer: Bay: *Jazzsteps Magazine* / numerous (Monthly, 1998)

6. Book: *"Writing for Pleasure and Profit"* (published, 2011) Founder: The Writing School.com (self-study — home study program to help people to write)

7. Music writing projects (3 thinking, Mal Sharpe, etc.)

8. Other magazine articles published, Hundreds — *Design Journal, Red Herring,* etc...

9. Baudelaire Book: *"Life in Paris",* Blue Matrix Productions (2012)

10. Academic Contributing Writer. *Bay Area Music Magazine,* many articles

11. Book *"Media Tipping Points, PhD Dissertation",* Blue Matrix Productions (2012)

12. *International Herald Tribune* Article: "Maybe the problem isn't the Gap Filler" 8/20/05

13. Book *"The Zodiac Project"* Blue Matrix Productions (published, 2012)

14. Book *"Paris Hotel Market Study",* Blue Matrix Productions (published, 2012)

15. Book *"London Hotel Market Study",* Blue Matrix Productions (published, 2012)

16. Book *"Chasing The Carrott. Launching the Dot Com Company",* Blue Matrix Productions (published, 2012)

17. Book *"Reflections",* Selected Poetry, Blue Matrix Productions (published, 2011)

18. Book *"Destinations",* Photographs, Travels and Cities, Blue Matrix Productions (2012)

19. Book *"Collections of Articles",* 1990-2010, Blue Matrix Productions (2012)

See website: http://www.mdg-consultants.com

Part Seven
Cities: "The Earth Explored"

Subconscious Concept: Cities where I have lived or spent considerable time studying the culture, language, arts, way of life, people, and images. Focusing on the who? what?, where? how? and why? And their relationship to The Zodiac Project-each cities relevance from a energy, life journey perspective, historical perspective, etc.

Concious Reality: Exhibitions, photographic and cultural survey, and workshops on how others can understand the places they have lived or visited, as it relates to their life journey/energy.

Cities: (Status: All of the following have been lived in)

1. Paris, France
2. San Francisco, California
3. Washington, DC
4. New York, New York
5. Rio, Brazil
6. Bali, Indonesia
7. Burgundy, France
8. Belize, Bahamas and Bermuda
9. Cozumel, Mexico
10. Buenos Aires, Argentina
11. Sydney, Auckland, Fiji
12. Cape Town, South Africa

See website: http://www.mdg-consultants.com

Part Eight
Photographs

Subconscious Concept: 12 Black and white or color images, exhibition format that best represent the 12 energies associated with the project. Actual photographs taken during my journey. May illustrate or connect events, places, experiences, people, spiritual awareness, happiness/compassion, etc.

Concious Reality: "A Visual Essay": (12) distinct images that depict the "cycle of life", this can later be expanded as photographic essay for a coffee table book, with text and commentary for The Zodiac Project Foundation Exhibition.

First exhibition: "Patterns and Light", Soucy, France (2010) and images in "Reflections" and "Destinations" books (2012).

See website: http://www.mdg-consultants.com

Part Nine
Teachings/People:

Subconscious Concept: Outside of immediate loves ones or family, who are the twelve most important people in my life (in the world), i. e.: incredible, inspirational people who I have met and who have influenced and enhanced my life journey.

Who are the 12 most important people in your life? How do recognize them?

Concious Reality: Profile/illustrations/meaningful reflection of their impact and influence on my journey and why...

The people...

1. My Father: William, 1922–1997
2. President Bill Clinton: President of the United States
3. Sting: Entertainer/Performer/Humanitarian
4. Wayne Shorter: Composer/Jazz Artist
5. The many jazz giants I have met/worked with/played music with/admired: Joe Henderson, Art Framer, Rufus Ried, Marc Levine, McCoy Tyner, Harold Land, Billy Higgins, Joe Lovano, etc, etc.
6. Nancy: A good spirit and example
7. Christopher Reeves: "Superman"
8. Arnold Schwar"zen"egger: Actor/Governor of California
9. President Gerald Ford, President of the United States
10. Dr. William Palank — my best friend, "wing man"
11. Anne-Lyse, the love of my life
12. Jaike William-Pierre, my son, who changed my life forever...

Part Ten
"Les Colours" and "Les Notes"

Subconscious Concept: I have been teaching university color courses all of the world and playing music professionally for almost 30 years. How are these two artistic mediums related? What influence do they have on our perceptions of our world? How do they influence us, like the other parts, subconsciously or consciously?

Concious Reality: Book/Music/Workshops: the colors and the notes: "12 on 12", music /color exercise workbook/with illustrations: i. e. 3D "Canvas"

Concept detail: 12 musical notes defined as colors:
1. C: medium yellow: both warm and cool
2. G: medium blue: more towards cool
3. D: medium purple: cool
4. A: warm red: cool
5. E: red: cool
6. B: light blue: cool
7. Gb: blue-green/F#: green-blue
8. Db: purple: warm, or red/blue, C#: light yellow: cool*
9. Ab: wine: warm, or red/blue, G#: blue: cool: wine/red
10. Eb: red-voilet: warm, D#: purple/blue: cool
11. Bb: light, warm, red/wine, A#: light: cool: red/wine
12. F: Green: warm, not cool

*notes also shown in enharmonics

Part Eleven
"Les Femmes"

Subconscious Concept: Who are/were the 12 most important women in PG life? (Who are the most important women in your life?) Why? What signs are they? What about their relationships to the other parts?

Concious Reality: Photographs/bios/explanations of the 12 most important women in my life journey... (for women in their Zodiac Framework "Energy Map"... it will be titled: "Les Hommes")

Les Femmes:
1. Patricia: my mother
2. Linda: my first love experience: virginity
3. Nancy: The Ballerina
4. Dee: "cancer strikes"
5. Shana: "the illegal Danish girl"
6. Katherine: "cancer strikes again"
7. Nicola: "South Africa Apartheid"
8. Cindy: "loss of trust"
9. Vanessa: the 22-year-old Italian "Shrink"
10. Jennifer: the "senator's" wife
11. Babou: The ecologist
12. Anne-Lyse, mother of my child and only true love...

Part Twelve:
The Zodiac Foundation

Subconscious Concept: This is the culmination of this 12-part project which has developed a "wayfinding "process for others to follow. This becomes the springboard concept to launch what I would hope would follow as the Zodiac Foundation.

For now, the Zodiac Foundation detail is conceptual, as I don't want to detail this too much right now, knowing it will evolve and flexibility is key. The Zodiac Foundation will author a Charter and set goals and objectives.

Concious Reality: "Evolutionary Energy Map", development and site selection of The Zodiac Center location for workshops, seminars, fundraising administration, infrastructure, interactive website, workbooks, game, fellowships, study, outreach programs, etc.

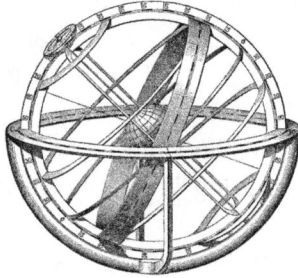

VIII. Observations

If you remember, at the beginning of this book, I asked you a question...

"Are you happy?"

I think I can safely say that not that many people will be able to reply with a resounding yes. Most people are unable to say their life is everything they had hoped it would be. What is it that causes us so much pain? What is it that is going on in the world that prevents so many people from simply being happy?

And so now we are back where we started. Can there ever be a single solution that can apply to all people on the globe, that everyone can be convinced of, and that is so simple that everyone can understand it?

In fact, I have found the answer, and it is just this: and I will repeat it again here. We are nothing more than an assemblage of different types of energies, or molecules. We exist, from the moment we are conceived in our mothers' womb until we pass onto to another life, as "energy".

From a physical perspective, humans are energy. When you finally realize this you will start to look at the world a whole new way.

Energy applies to all people.

"Energy that is moving is like water in a river", you can feel it.

Moving, changing, flowing-this is what life is about-energy.

The Zodiac Project: Key Points

- Based on one man's life experience, awareness and exploration, The Zodiac Project outlines and presents in (12) artistic mediums, a "wayfinding" framework for discovery of the "parallel world", the world of every human's essence, the world that connects the conscious to subconscious.

- The basic premise is that everybody already is a "Master" and "Perfect", and, merely has to connect with their own parallel world and potential.

- The Zodiac Project framework outlines an "Energy Map", a step-by-step approach for personal "wayfinding", a method for all people to understand their own lives, build an awareness of their own (parallel) world, a method to understand their decisions, their interactions with people, events, etc.

- The Zodiac Project is the only "holistic", personal, spiritual, life-journey framework in existence.

- The Zodiac Project has been developed to explore the essence of the 12 zodiac signs from both a Western and Chinese astrological perspective.

- The Zodiac Project provides an artistic and commercially viable launching vehicle for development of marketable products and events which guarantees a significant (ROI) and economically justifies the entire project.

- Worldwide interest in astrological signs, spirituality, energy, religion, the numerous artistic segments (music, paintings, architecture, etc. and, this market is growing, increasingly, as world events and personal need for discovery takes on a higher priority.

- And finally, with completion of The Zodiac Project... a "place", i. e. The Zodiac Foundation will be created where anyone can personally visualize, listen, explore, test, interact with the different parts of the project and, where one can learn how to develop and understand their own life cycle, or, "Energy Map".

I sincerely wish you good energy as you continue your life journey...

and ask you: "Isn't it time you had an "Energy Map" of your own?"

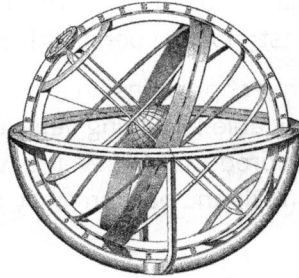

IX. Zodiac Foundation

In eight years The Zodiac Project has completed all but (2) parts of the (12) "Parts", and has been selling Zodiac Project commercial products, to "customers" worldwide. I invision a staff of (12) people, engaged in management, development, research, administration, workshops and distribution. The Zodiac Project will have offices located in 12 cities. Paris will be the Headquarters for the Project.

Realistic?

I think it will already exceed my humble expectations, it has already created such energy and inspiration, that people from all of the world already benefit from its' principles, practices and philosophy.

The key feature of The Zodiac Project is that it will also continue to evolve, i. e. have it's own "Cycle of Life". Also, as The Zodiac Project process, or, framework for the "Energy Map" has hands-on customer use and interest, resulting soon in a game, workbook, seminars, philosophy, movie, TV show, podcasts (additional mediums are available) and Zodiac Foundation.

The Zodiac Foundation is for enhancement and teaching and exploring. Teaching this "wayfinding" process for every person to find connections between the conscious and subconscious journey for their own life, the life of others and the world around them.

Mission statement

- The Zodiac Project will create and develop products and services specifically related to the "Energy Map" and "Cycle of Life".

- Develop a network on centers with artists and boards and then, via distribution channels:
    - Internet
    - Workshops
    - Word of Mouth
    - Collateral Materials
    - Concerts
    - Exhibitions
    - CD/DVD's
    - Books
    - Seminars
    - Game
    - Movie
    - Etc.

Other media vehicles and products as developed and approved by the Foundation.

Values and Goals

- **Ethically:** The Zodiac Project will only have the highest standards.

- **Energy Network:** The search for Sponsors and how they will be selected is critical in the development and overall process.

- **Outreach:** The search for Creative and Advisory Board members and their input to the project as a whole, is critical.

- **Customers/Clients:** This concept becomes a way of reaching large segments of the world's population, persons who are seeking realistic, professional and holistic answers to the meaning or purpose of life and real happiness.

X. The Zodiac Foundation: Goals and Objectives

There is currently not a similar project envisioned or completed based on the same fundamental principles. Considering the aggregate size of the project: i. e. artists, non-artists, patrons and customers/clients, where there already exists a passing or passionate interest in astrological signs, spirituality, energy, religion, numerous artistic market segments (music, painting, readers, architecture, photographers, etc.) and related "life journey" interest groups, i. e.: think: "What Color is my Parachute? "and "The Artists Way" market groups.

The Zodiac Foundation will be overseen by notable business, creative and advisory boards who have been selected to assist with guidance, feedback and promotion of the project as it develops.

Financial Requirements

The following outline the financial funding requirements for each of the (2) two Zodiac Foundation phases. The phases are envisioned seperately in this manner, as funding vehicle for launching the initial parts of the project, whereby, illustrating the fundelmental energy concepts and, creating an artistic direction and momentum for the remaining portions of the project.

Phase One

The Zodiac Project requires what is termed: **"Initial Sponsor Funding"**, in the amount of: $270,000.00 (US) in order to achieve the project "milestones" and to bring to market "deliverables" as outlined for these two parts i. e. to develop, acquire, negotiate, contract, assemble the Zodiac "team" for management and artistic and creative structure, establish workspace and offices, out-fitting, and other project related equipment and supplies.

Equally as important, Phase One will include funds for efforts to refine and complete the remaining portions of the Zodiac Foundation.

The Zodiac Foundation will require the services of consultants to develop detailed market analyses, accounting and projections, estimates of revenue/costs, etc, as well as typical exhibits and forecasting documents.

In addition, approximately $30,000.00 US which is received as a result of the first phase of the Zodiac Foundation (i. e.: through sales of CDs, events, exhibitions, etc.) and additional sponsorships.

Funding will be allocated as follows:

- Artists' contracts, execution, researching, archiving, and creative development
- Recording, Mixing, Duplication, Artwork, and Formatting, etc.
- "Concert" and "Exhibition" services, marketing and communications
- Printing and Collaterals
- Studio/office Space: Equipment and Supplies/Phones/Internet/Computer, etc
- Fees: Legal/Accounting/Licenses
- Set-up, Artistic Management/Business Plan refinement

Total Phase One: $300,000.00 (US)

Phase Two

Phase Two funding requirements will be developed with the assistance of the various boards and after development of the Zodiac Foundation.

**Estimated Investor Funding for Phase Two:
$2,000,000.00 (US)**

Why is The Zodiac Foundation Important: SWOT

STRENGTHS

The world is both consciously and unconsciously seeking "answers" to possible links between psychology and science.

- Cycle of Life: Astrology has been studied for many years, and is increasingly becoming a multi-billion dollar industry.

- Energy: fundamental, is the notion of "energy" (positive and negative). What is it? Why do we experience it? How can we learn to use it? Connect with it? Etc.

- Dedication: The Zodiac Foundation is 100% committed to this project. Project is currently on going, compositions still being written, architectural projects are being built, videos are being created, etc.

- Belief in Journey: What is it? Why do we experience it? Answers to questions? Why does religion work? Because people want to have faith

WEAKNESSES

- The author personally may not have enough time to finish... (he is currently 58 years young, when you have these moments of enlightenment and see these kind of answers. I. e. "Holistic" answers for your life, you wonder... maybe, it's time I move on... the project is estimated take between 2–10 years.

- "This is What I do" — other artists who have said that.
- People who think "Zodiac" is too... "spiritual"... "touchy-feely"... cliché

MARKET OPPORTUNITIES

- The author has actually been living this process, (i. e. the "Pendulum" screenplay was written in 1993, not something that was recently conceived).
- "Cycle of Life" process of "wayfinding", is applicable to all people.
- (12) personality/people/energy types. People already have a genuine interest in self-development seminars, workshops, etc. for discovering things about their potential, what makes them happy, etc.

Expertise, new and improved method, concept, aggregate market demand in a cross-section of consumers areas, i. e. $30 Billion in US alone, Europe, World markets expanding as well as increasing demand in those areas, pricing strategy (TBD), reputation of principals, participating artists and the various creative and advisory boards, image, trends.

MARKET THREATS

Competing music and art projects, astrological and spiritual commercial interests in the increasing world markets. (Overall market depth is enormous) which shouldn't be a factor.

100's videos, how-to guides, reach the market each month and are gobbled up by the public.

The Zodiac Project name, ideas, principles can and will be copied by opportunists. However, no one can really copy a work of art without it being a "fake", (or the resultant being one step removed from the original). The Framework Process, Foundation and "Energy Map" are copyrighted and secured accordingly. Both in the US and European Markets.

XI. Zodiac Sponsorship

Why would you be interested in becoming a Sponsor of The Zodiac Foundation?

As a Phase One, Project Sponsor, you will participate in the following:

- Assisting in the launching of a significant milestone about an artist's life work and The Zodiac Foundation.

- Based on your principal contribution, you would realize 20-30% return on investment in just under two years.

- You will have an opportunity to be instrumental and actively contribute to the development of the Zodiac Foundation. Resulting in both, economical and artistic (spiritual) returns.

- You will have the option of an equity position during the development of The Zodiac Foundation.

CATEGORIES OF SPONSOR TYPES

- **Financial Sponsor: "Active"** — Member of The Zodiac Advisory Board: Management/Operations
- **Financial Sponsor: "Supporter/Patron"** — Lends name/Resources/Funds: The Zodiac Advisory Board: Artist/Business Network
- **Creative Sponsor: "Active"** — Member of The Zodiac Project Creative Board: Artists: Contributes Funds
- **Creative Sponsor** Lends Resources/funds-name only
- **Contributing Sponsor** Resources/Funds only
- **Volunteer Sponsor** Volunteers time/energy

THE ZODIAC PROJECT MANAGEMENT BOARDS

- **Creative Advisory Board (two types)** — Active and Financial Contributor — both promote and endorse project
- **Business/Development Advisory Board (two types)** Active and Title only — intellectual asset contributor

Are you reading this to become a **Sponsor**?

Are you reading this to become a **Creative Team Member**?

Are you reading this to become an **Advisory Board Member**?

Do you want to learn more about **The Zodiac Project**, assistance with your own journey, cycle of life... Energy Map?

Are you considering investing in **The Zodiac Project**?

CONTACT US

For answers to your questions and to learn more about how to become a member or advisor, or, funding options or donation programs as well as additional Zodiac Foundation Information, can be obtained by contacting:

THE ZODIAC PROJECT AND FOUNDATION:
CONTACT INFORMATION / PROJECT DIRECTORY

Legal name and status of business	The Zodiac Project
Director	Philip Gordon Creative Director
Address of main offices	**France** 2 Rue Despaty, Voisines FR 89260 **USA** 2995 Woodside Road, Suite 400 Woodside, CA 94065
Main telephone	+33 (0) 621 21 13 55
Main e-mail	Designanalysispm@aol.com
Official Website	http://www.mdg-consultants.com